FORGOTTEN BONES

UNCOVERING a SLAVE CEMETERY

LOIS MINER HUEY

M MILLBROOK PRESS • MINNEAPOLIS

For Hartgen Archeological Associates, especially Matt Kirk, Karen Hartgen, and Corey McQuinn, and for the New York State Museum, especially Lisa Anderson and Gay Malin
—L.M.H.

PHOTO ACKNOWLEDGMENTS

The images in this book are used with the permission of: © iStockphoto.com/Tarek El Sombati (dirt); © Independent Picture Service (graph paper); Courtesy of "Hartgen Archeological Associates Inc.", p. 5 (all), 6, 7, 9, 13 (all), 14 (all), 15 (all), 17, 18; © Old Paper Studios/Alamy, p. 10 (top); New York State Archives. New York (State), Education Dept. Division of Archives and History, Photographs of historic sites and structures, 1936–1963, Series A0245-77. Box 1, Albany County, No. 9., p. 10; Mid-Manhattan Picture Collection/Slavery — United States/The New York Public Library, Astor, Lenox and Tilden Foundations, p. 11; © Albany Institute of History & Art, p. 12; © Manuel Velasco/E+/Getty Images, p. 16; Courtesy of Paul R. Huey, Division for Historic Preservation, New York State Office of Parks, Recreation and Historic Preservation, p. 16 (bottom); © Laura Westlund/Independent Picture Service, pp. 19, 22, 35; Courtesy New York State Museum, Albany, NY, p. 21 (all), 23, 25, 33 (all); © Nucleus Medical Art/Visuals Unlimited, Inc., p. 24; © Andy Chopping/ MOLA, p. 26; © Ermakoff/Science Source, p. 27; © Gay Malin, pp. 30, 32; Frances M. Roberts/Newscom, p. 36 (all); © Bettmann/CORBIS, p. 37; © African Burial Ground Project /Howard University and GSA/Institute for Biology/College of William and Mary, Williamsburg, VA., pp. 38, 42; Mid-Manhattan Picture Collection/Slavery — United States, Miriam and Ira D. Wallach Division of Art, Prints and Photographs, The New York Public Library, Astor, Lenox and Tilden Foundations, p. 39; © Stephen Chernin/Getty Images, p. 40; © North Wind Picture Archives/Alamy, p. 46; Stephen Cernin/EPA/Newscom, p. 49 (top left); © Paul Huey, p. 49 (top); National Park Service, p. 49 (bottom).

Front cover: Courtesy of Hartgen Archeological Associates Inc.

Jacket flaps: © iStockphoto.com/Tarek El Sombati (dirt).

Back cover: Courtesy of "Hartgen Archeological Associates Inc. (sketch); © Independent Picture Service (graph paper).

Millbrook Press
A division of Lerner Publishing Group, Inc.
241 First Avenue North
Minneapolis, MN 55401 USA

For reading levels and more information, look up this title at www.lernerbooks.com.

Main body text set in Chaparral Pro Regular 12/16.
Typeface provided by Adobe Systems.

Library of Congress Cataloging-in-Publication Data

Huey, Lois Miner.
    Forgotten bones: uncovering a slave cemetery/ by Lois Miner Huey.
    pages cm
    Includes bibliographical references and index.
    ISBN 978–1–4677–3393–9 (library binding : alkaline paper)
    ISBN 978–1–4677–6300–4 (eBook)
    1. African Americans—Northeastern States—Antiquities—Juvenile literature. 2. Slave cemeteries—Northeastern States—Juvenile literature. 3. African American cemeteries—Northeastern States—Juvenile literature. 4. Slaves—Tombs—Northeastern States—Juvenile literature. 5. Human remains (Archaeology)—Northeastern States—Juvenile literature. 6. Slaves—Northeastern States—History—Juvenile literature. 7. African Americans—Northeastern States—History—Juvenile literature. 8. Slavery—Northeastern States—History—Juvenile literature. 9. Northeastern States—Antiquities—Juvenile literature. I. Title.
    E185.9.H83 2016
    306.3'620974—dc23   2014009379

Manufactured in the United States of America

1 – DP – 7/15/15

CONTENTS

INTRODUCTION

NEAR ALBANY, NEW YORK, JUNE 2005

The backhoe's teeth bit into the pavement, shattering the silence of early morning with a loud roar. Skies were clear, and the sun shone brightly. The day would be hot. Because it was Sunday, businesses were closed. Workers could use the backhoe to cut across the paved driveway, dig a trench, lay sewer pipe, and fill the trench again without disturbing workweek traffic. At least that was the plan.

The backhoe scooped up dirt and dumped it on a growing mound of debris. Soil, rocks, and gravel spilled down the sides. A round object rolled down the pile and landed at the boots of a workman. He bent and picked it up. With a gloved hand, he brushed it off. He turned it over and over. Suddenly, he found himself staring into eye sockets and cupping the hinges of a jaw. This was a skull.

The workman wanted to know more about the skull, but he had to get back to work. He carefully wrapped it in a handkerchief and laid it in the shade of some nearby trees. Then he returned to the backhoe.

Not long after, town historian Kevin Franklin arrived at the site. He'd heard about the digging and wanted to take a closer look.

"Find anything interesting?" Franklin yelled over the noise of the backhoe.

"Just found a skull," the worker yelled back. He pointed in the direction of the trees.

Franklin promptly picked up the skull and removed it from the handkerchief. The workers shut down the machines to take a lunch break. Before eating, the men gathered around Franklin.

"I was called to this same place in 1998 when a female skeleton in a coffin was found," Franklin said later. "So [I knew] this new skull might mean there were more skeletons there. We needed to call in archaeologists to investigate this properly."

Franklin reached for his cell phone and started making calls. He contacted the police, an engineering company, some town officials, and a representative from the state historic preservation office. All the while, questions about the skull and the site formed. Is this skull a stray find? Where is the rest of the skeleton? Was the person murdered? Are there more bones? Could this be the site of a lost cemetery?

Slamming car doors and loud voices soon filled the air. The police, looking for obvious signs of trauma, studied the skull. They noted none. They also had no record of a missing person. They didn't believe the site was a crime scene, but the coroner had to make that determination, and he was busy and at least an hour away.

Then four archaeologists, scientists who study historic people and cultures, arrived. They worked for Hartgen Archeological Associates, a company with expertise in excavating historic sites. The engineering firm had called them. The four scientists dashed over to look at the skull. Erin Kline, a bioarchaeologist, inspected it especially closely. After several minutes, she told everyone

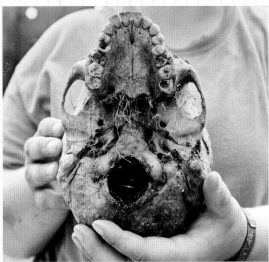

What Bioarchaeologists Do

Bioarchaeologists are scientists who study human remains. They specialize in excavated bones. Bioarchaeologists look at details such as the length and width of the bones, the appearance of bones where muscles were attached, and the overall condition of the bones. These observations reveal the age, sex, race, and health of the people before they died.

the skull was very old. She estimated the person had died one hundred or more years ago. She added that judging by the bone structure, the skull was probably from an African American person.

The four archaeologists jumped into the trench and began investigating the layers of soil. The police promptly ordered the archaeologists out of the hole. No one was allowed to do anything until the coroner came and did his work. Only the coroner could officially declare the site a place for study and not a crime scene.

The archaeologists returned to the skull, taking it and settling in the shade of the trees, out of the hot sun.

How Archaeologists Read Soil Layers

Soil builds in layers over time. Wind, worms, and human activity all play a role in changing the layers of the land. Archaeologists carefully scrape away each level of dirt using small tools. They study artifacts such as glass shards and iron nails and bone pieces. Artifacts help archaeologists understand the culture of the different peoples who lived at the site. Archaeologists also study the soil itself. When someone in the past shifted the soil, it would have changed color or texture or both. So when they find dark stains or a change in the type of soil, archaeologists know some kind of activity has taken place. They dig these features separately to figure out what happened.

Three hours later, the coroner finally arrived. He talked with the police and to the archaeologists. He looked at the skull, and he too recognized it was old. He determined the site was not a crime scene.

The archaeologists, trowels in hand, eagerly returned to the trench. They scraped the soil along its sides and bottom. Soon they found dark stains indicating the presence of at least two more graves.

Perhaps there were more graves still. Town officials agreed to postpone construction so the archaeologists could look for more graves.

Archaeologists from Hartgen Archeological Associates stand in a trench near where a human skull was discovered near Albany, New York, in 2005.

CHAPTER ONE

EXCAVATIONS

The archaeologists returned to the site early the next morning. They asked the backhoe operator to scrape off approximately 2 feet (61 centimeters) of soil from the rest of the trench. Then the archaeologists got to work. They shoveled, scraped, and brushed off the dirt. They planted orange flags to mark dark patches. Dark soil indicated graves where burials had occurred. The team found thirteen discolored areas. Above the graves, they found a few artifacts that had been manufactured in the 1800s. This meant someone had probably dug the graves earlier than the 1800s.

Pulling out measuring tapes and notebooks, the archaeologists recorded the positions of the orange flags on a map. They spread black plastic over the top of the trench to protect the graves from the weather. Then they shoveled dirt over the plastic to discourage curious people and animals from disturbing the site.

Could the sewer project avoid these graves and leave them in peace? The town engineers considered alternate plans, but the project was too far along to change now. The skeletons needed to be removed. The archaeologists began writing a proposal describing how they would accomplish this task. The archaeologists also outlined how they planned to conduct additional research to try to answer the important question of who had been buried here. The team wanted to check documents and maps to find out whether the area had ever been a cemetery. Franklin and two historians from Albany's African American community reviewed old records. They studied maps and deeds that showed who had owned the land over the years. They interviewed people familiar with the history of the area.

The archaeologists planted orange flags to mark the areas they planned to excavate.

No one remembered a cemetery where the trench was, and the old maps didn't show one. If the spot had been a cemetery at one time, why wasn't it on any of the maps?

Important clues came from further research. Older maps and land deeds showed this land had once been owned by the Schuylers, a family who had acquired a large farm there and owned it until 1910. Other documents revealed a key detail: the Schuylers had owned slaves.

These burials were on what had been the Schuyler farm. The Schuyler family cemetery was on the farm as well, but it was located much closer to the main house. The graves there were clearly marked with headstones. These newly discovered graves were far away from the house, and they weren't marked in any way. Could these graves be part of a slave cemetery?

The archaeologists knew of only two slave cemeteries in the North: one discovered and excavated in New York City in 1991 and another in Portsmouth, New Hampshire, in 2003. If the Albany site was a slave burial ground, the information from the Schuyler farm burials could be added to what was learned from the other two. This would help paint a more complete picture about the lives of slaves in the North.

> If the spot had been a cemetery at one time, why wasn't it on any of the maps?

Many people think slavery existed only in the South. In reality, the North had many slaves for a time. Historians who study slavery point out that the practice varied in the two regions. Northern farms were smaller than their southern counterparts. If white northerners owned slaves, they didn't typically have many. But the North did benefit from the widespread use of slaves in the South. The crops the southern slaves planted and harvested, particularly cotton, were the raw materials northerners used in their factories.

What was life like for slaves in the North? Most lived on small farms or in cities. Usually each household had only one or two slaves. They lived in the same house as their enslavers and worked side by side with them or under their direct supervision. Few records were kept about the slaves. Slaves in the North lived and died, their contributions forgotten or ignored. Their cemeteries were disregarded and built over. Little information about their lives is known compared to the amount of information about slaves and slavery in the South where slavery was widespread and lasted longer as a way of life.

The Schuyler family farmhouse as it looked in 1941 (below). Philip Schuyler (right) spent part of his childhood on the farm. As an adult, he represented New York State in the US Senate from 1788 to 1791 and 1797 to 1798.

Slavery in the United States

Slavery was legal in parts of what is now the United States for more than three hundred years, and many slaves faced horrific treatment at the hands of traders and owners. The first slaves arrived in America in 1619, and tens of thousands followed. Most slaves who lived and died in colonial America were people from West Africa or their descendants. West Africans were kidnapped as part of the Atlantic slave trade. By 1799 almost twenty-six thousand enslaved people lived in the state of New York alone, most of them in New York City. Similar numbers existed in other northern colonies and states, including Pennsylvania and New Jersey. Both whites and blacks in the North began to demand that slavery be outlawed. Vermont abolished slavery in 1777, making it the first state to legally recognize that owning another human being is wrong. New York began abolishing slavery in 1799 by declaring that children born to slaves were free. New York abolished all slavery in 1827.

States in the South, on the other hand, held on to slavery. The reasons for this are complex. Southern plantation owners often believed slave labor was essential for the continued existence of these large farms. And some whites believed black people were not capable of living on their own. The conflict between the northern and southern perspectives on slavery became one of the major causes of the American Civil War (1861–1865). Toward the end of that war, President Abraham Lincoln signed the Emancipation Proclamation, which abolished slavery in the South on January 1, 1863. Slavery was officially abolished throughout the country when the Thirteenth Amendment to the US Constitution was adopted on December 18, 1865.

New York City slave harbor, circa 1730

An account of the horses black Cattel & Sheep
now upon ye farme of the flats april 12: 1711
taken up from marke Delemont Bowmaster
of ye flatts,

17 working horses or mares to ye best of his
knowledge that were in being & workt
Last fall — whereof one Sorrill horse att
Schuyler

3 of 3 year old
1 of 4 year old
4 of 2 years old
2 year eling Colts
2 yearly fillys

14 Cows of wch Seven
4 heffers
5 oxen
1 Bull
6 Calfs of a year Old

23 Sheep
17 young Lambs

5 Sows
1 Bore
14 or 15 Piggs

Account of negros & negrowomen

One negro Called Jacob
one ditto Called Charles
one ditto Called Peter
one ditto Called Tham
one do Called Anthony
one negro woman Called mary
one ditto Called Bettie

Inventary of ye reall Estate &c belongd to Philip
Schuyler & margaret his wife both deceasd taken
by their Children this 17th day of April 1711

The farme called ye flatts wth ye Island thereunto
belonging
The farm over ag.t it called formerly Constapleury
The Plantation adjoyning to ye farm called
flatts Commonly child written plantihon all
Lying in ye mannor Rensselaerswyk
2 houses & Lotts Lying in Albany in the Jonker
street whereof ye Deceasd Philip Schuyler
& marg. Schuyler deceasd
a house & lott Lying in Pearl Street between
Johann Cuylers & abraham Cuylers in ye S. Kitty
a Small Pasture upon ye road as ye go to ye
Old fort

This list includes horses, cattle,
sheep, and slaves on the Schuyler
farm on April 12, 1711.

Most slaves couldn't read or write and didn't leave written accounts about themselves. Details about their daily lives, their living conditions, their health, and their treatment are minimal. The four archaeologists working at the site near Albany suggested in their proposal that studying the bones could provide this information.

Other important questions emerged about the Schuyler farm project. What would happen to the skeletons once they were removed from the ground? Would they be reburied and forgotten again? Would they be tucked away in a museum storeroom? Would they be studied? Would analysis help bring honor to the slaves' lives and deaths?

Lisa Anderson, a bioarchaeologist at the New York State Museum, expressed interest in the bones. When a skeleton had been found near the Schuyler farm location in 1998, she and others from the museum studied it. Because of that experience and because the newly discovered remains were likely part of the same burial ground, Anderson became the lead researcher on the project at the museum. With a plan in place, excavations could begin.

WORK BEGINS

Three weeks after the burial ground's accidental discovery, Erin Kline arrived at the site with a crew and a truckload of equipment. She brought shovels, trowels, rulers, cameras, root cutters, buckets, and screens to filter the dirt for any artifacts missed by the archaeologists. Kline's team carefully pulled up the black plastic that covered the hole. Some of the crew settled down next to the orange flags she and the other archaeologists had placed during their first visit. Others set up cameras and filter screens.

They worked quietly, well aware of the importance of the excavation. Archaeologist Matt Kirk said, "Field work on human remains is a quiet process, almost meditative. The work has to be careful and meticulous. And you are always aware that these people once were alive."

The backhoe sat nearby. Its presence was a constant reminder the sewer line remained unfinished. Hot, rainy days made the archaeologists' work challenging and miserable.

Researchers set up canopies to protect people and bones from hot sun and rain.

Dark soil hints at the presence of a grave. With trowels and brushes, researchers carefully remove the soil around the coffins and bones.

The team erected small, blue tents over the site so they could keep working in rainy weather.

The crew excavated each burial shaft with trowels. When the team found wooden coffin lids, workers used brushes to sweep off the dirt. Most of the wood was deteriorated, but the crew made scale drawings of what remained. They photographed each partial lid, removed it, and saved the wood. They also dug out soil from alongside each coffin to make room for workers to kneel and work.

Next, the archaeologists used small tools and brushes to remove sand and gravel that had fallen inside the rotting coffins and covered the skeletons. Workers frequently sprayed water on the exposed bones and wood. If the bones and wood dried out too fast, they would split into pieces. The workers wanted to prevent splintering.

After fully exposing each skeleton, the workers photographed and made a scale drawing of it. These photos and sketches provided a record of each find as it was uncovered. The workers suspected the site was a slave cemetery, but they couldn't rule out other possibilities. American Indian cemeteries hadn't been marked either, and these same archaeologists had excavated several of those sites, which had been in the path of construction projects.

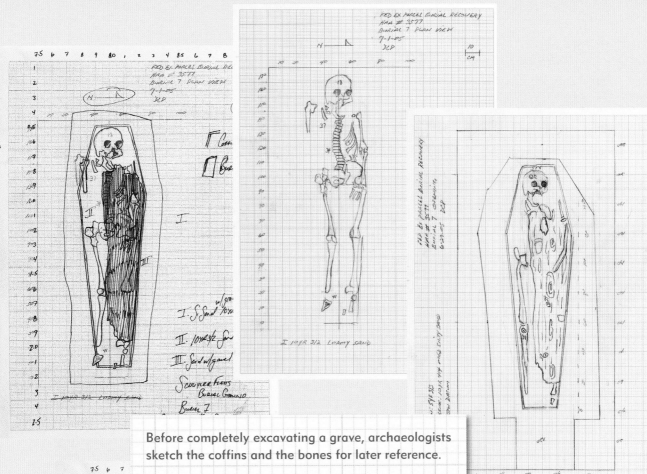

Before completely excavating a grave, archaeologists sketch the coffins and the bones for later reference.

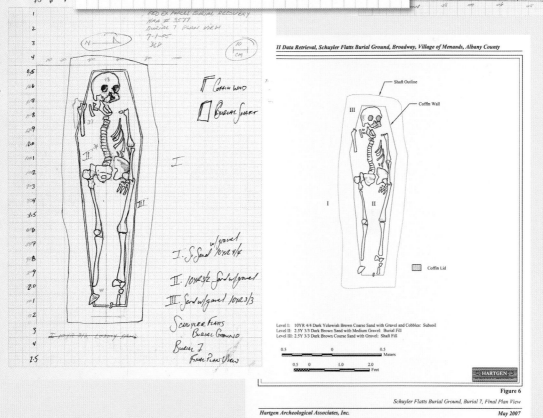

II Data Retrieval, Schuyler Flatts Burial Ground, Broadway, Village of Menands, Albany County

Shaft Outline

Coffin Wall

Coffin Lid

Level I: 10YR 4/4 Dark Yellowish Brown Coarse Sand with Gravel and Cobbles: Subsoil
Level II: 2.5Y 3/3 Dark Brown Sand with Medium Gravel: Burial Fill
Level III: 2.5Y 3/3 Dark Brown Coarse Sand with Gravel: Shaft Fill

HARTGEN

Figure 6

Schuyler Flatts Burial Ground, Burial 7, Final Plan View

Hartgen Archeological Associates, Inc.   May 2007

Workers recovered thirteen bodies at the Albany site. Twelve were in their graves. One was in the pile of dirt the backhoe had dug up. The workers on Kline's team speculated about each person's sex, age, and cause of death. With Kline's help, each worker recorded these thoughts and possible answers in notes. Sometimes a hunch from the person in the field helps answer a question in the lab.

THE COFFINS

Five adults had been buried in coffins with six corners, the common style in the 1700s. Two of the children had been buried in these hexagonal boxes as well. One adult and four other children had been placed in coffins with four corners. The different coffin sizes and shapes suggested that each coffin was built especially for the body inside and that special care was taken for each person's remains. Later analysis would show the wood used to make the coffins was from a tree common to the area, the eastern white pine.

The children's small coffins contained as many or more nails than the adult coffins, which were larger. One infant's coffin had been built using forty nails. At the time the coffin was built, blacksmiths made nails by hand. Creating them was time-consuming and costly. The presence of so many nails in a child's coffin showed how much care the mourners took with children's burials. The nails themselves gave further clues about when the bodies had been buried. Machine-cut nails didn't come into wide use until after about 1790. No nails made by machine were present. This detail helped the archaeologists figure out the graves were made before about 1790.

Nail type, coffin shape, and wood used for coffins all give researchers clues about the approximate year of a burial. The nails at left are examples of handmade nails.

THE SHROUDS

Professionals of the twenty-first century prepare dead bodies for burial. In the 1700s, families did such work. Letters and diaries from the 1700s make it clear that women, both white and black, washed the dead and wrapped the bodies in a cloth called a shroud. The adult bodies discovered at Schuyler farm were wrapped in loose shrouds, fastened with a knot or a straight pin or two.

The children's bodies were wrapped in shrouds as well. But the shrouds were pinned much more tightly around the small bodies they encased. Archaeologists discovered twenty-five whole and partial pins with one child's skeleton. Like nails, pins at that time were made by hand and were expensive. Wrapping the children so firmly in shrouds before placing them in coffins suggested how much the grieving adults wanted to hug the children's bodies.

THE SKELETONS

Five of the skeletons were infants (under the age of one), and two were children under the age of ten. "The hardest burials to deal with were the children," team member Corey McQuinn said. "It was sad to see so many, and their bones were quite deteriorated. But we managed to get partial skeletons in each case." Three infant burials were in such poor condition, workers lifted them out as part of a block of soil. Researchers excavated these remains later in the state museum lab, where they could examine the tiny bones more clearly.

All the skeletons' heads faced east, the direction of the rising sun. This was common practice in both Africa and in early America. The belief was that eventually these people would rise from the dead and greet a new day. Many people associate this practice with Christianity, but it predates

The slaves buried their dead with their heads facing east. They believed that when their dead loved ones rose again, they would face a new day.

Christianity. For thousands of years, cultures around the world, including in West Africa, buried the dead this way.

The adults' hands lay alongside their bodies or were crossed over their hips. The positioning of hands over hips suggested the hands had once been tied together with a ribbon. The ribbon had deteriorated long ago.

Two adult skeletons were quite damaged. Tree roots had grown between the bones, separating and breaking many of them. One adult skeleton was very much intact, except it had no skull. The archaeologists were very pleased to discover that skeleton belonged to the skull the construction workers had found when working on the sewer project.

Mourners had not left artifacts with the bodies. This was typical of that time period for both blacks and whites. Leaving gifts on top of a coffin or grave was common in West Africa. However, the Schuyler farm slaves had by this time adopted the white custom of not leaving gifts. As the archaeologists finished excavating each grave, they removed the bones one by one. To protect them, workers carefully wrapped each bone in acid-free tissue paper and gently placed it into a labeled plastic bag. Then the archaeologists placed the bags in sealed plastic storage bins. The researchers treated the nails and pins in the same manner. The bins also contained the coffin wood the team had excavated. At the end of each day, the team took the plastic bins to the museum.

Even though many of the bones were deteriorated, the archaeologists carefully measured, excavated, preserved, and recorded all of them.

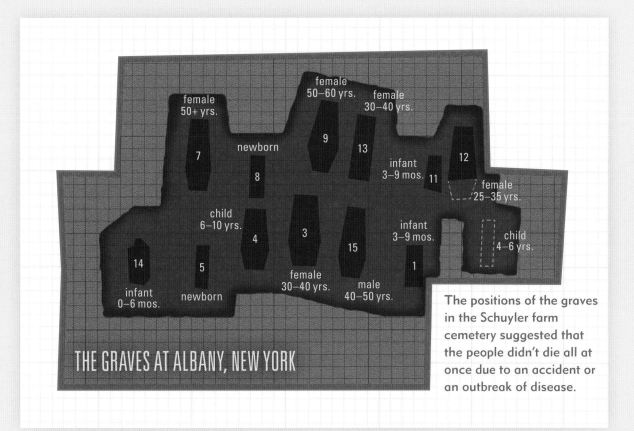

THE GRAVES AT ALBANY, NEW YORK

The positions of the graves in the Schuyler farm cemetery suggested that the people didn't die all at once due to an accident or an outbreak of disease.

WHAT THE CEMETERY LAYOUT REVEALED

Once the skeletons had been removed, the excavators studied the cemetery's layout. The graves formed two rows. Because burials were spaced differently within the rows, they clearly hadn't taken place at the same time. This detail was important. It meant these people hadn't died all at once from illness or an accident. Markers may have identified the graves at one time. If so, they had probably been made of wood that deteriorated long ago.

The location of Burial #2 (not shown on diagram) and the skeleton that had been found in 1998 suggested a third row of graves existed. Should the archaeologists look? One of the main reasons for the excavation was to prevent the bones from being destroyed by the sewer project. Graves in a possible third row lay outside the sewer line location and would be safe. Workers were reluctant to disturb graves without a good reason. In addition, the lack of time and money for the project helped everyone involved decide they would not excavate the probable third row of graves. Aware of the sensitive area, the state and town officials agreed that no construction projects would be allowed in that vicinity.

CHAPTER TWO

AT THE LAB

At the New York State Museum, workers began analyzing the skeletons to learn what they could from the forgotten bones. Measurements of bones would reveal the height, sex, and age of each person whose bones had been discovered at the site. Close examination might also yield information about his or her physical condition and even details about the daily lives of slaves at the Schuyler farm.

The first step for Anderson and Vanessa Dale was to prepare the bones for study. Anderson and Dale dried the bones very slowly, so they wouldn't split apart. Anderson explained, "When the burials arrived, Vanessa and I only removed the lids from the plastic boxes to let drying begin." The bones, still wrapped in their acid-free tissue paper, air-dried on trays. Eventually, Anderson and Dale opened the wrappings little by little and left the bones exposed. Slowly the bones dried, without splitting or splintering.

Most of the soil flaked off, but the researchers had to remove the rest. "We used no water and no scrubbing, just soft brushes," Anderson said. "We didn't want to cause any damage." Two high school students volunteered to help with this process. It took them about three months working with soft brushes to clean all the bones.

Once the bones were clean, the workers laid them out in their original order: head, chest, arms, and legs. Adding the woman's skeleton found in 1998 to the thirteen recent finds, fourteen skeletons were ready for the state museum staff to examine.

Researchers took careful measurements at the New York State Museum lab. These revealed whether the bones came from a man or a woman and the approximate age of the person.

INITIAL OBSERVATIONS

Anderson and Dale began studying the bones. They recorded what they saw on special fact sheets. They described the bones' conditions and the presence of any hair. Then they measured each bone. A woman's pelvis and hip bones are shaped differently than a man's. Measurements of pelvis and hip bones showed that six of the adults were women. One was a male. Other measurements confirmed the height and age of each person at the time of death. Anderson and Dale drew a color diagram of each skeleton that showed which bones were present and what the bones revealed.

SKELETAL STUDIES

Skull shapes and measurements helped establish ancestry. The bones belonged to people of African American descent. Typically the foreheads of African Americans are rounded, while the foreheads of European Americans are flattened. Usually African American jaws are a prominent feature on their faces, whereas those of European Americans are less pronounced. The nasal cavities of African Americans are normally wider than the nasal cavities of European Americans. Anderson knew the children were also African American because whites and blacks, even children, were not buried in the same cemeteries in the 1700s.

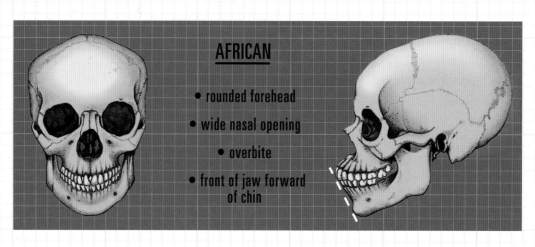

AFRICAN

- rounded forehead
- wide nasal opening
- overbite
- front of jaw forward of chin

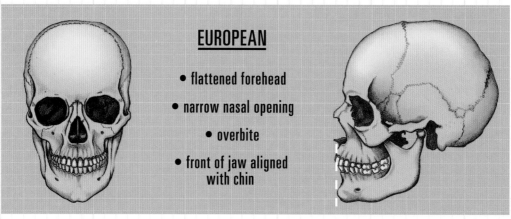

EUROPEAN

- flattened forehead
- narrow nasal opening
- overbite
- front of jaw aligned with chin

AGES AT DEATH

Seven skeletons were children. The youngest had died at birth. One may have lived to the age of ten. Their fragile bones were so small and deteriorated that Anderson and Dale couldn't determine the children's gender. Both black and white children during this time period often died young. People in this era didn't understand the causes of diseases, so they didn't follow practices that are common today, such as hand washing and sneezing into the crook of your bent arm. In addition, many medicines simply didn't exist, such as antibiotics to fight tuberculosis and immunizations to fight measles and smallpox, which were common and often deadly.

After careful examination, the researchers determined the youngest woman in the group died between the age of twenty-five and thirty-five. She may have developed an infection after giving birth, which was common in the 1700s. The oldest woman was considerably older than fifty. The male was between the ages of forty and fifty. The average age at death for both whites and blacks in the 1700s was about thirty. Because childhood mortality was high at that time, the average life expectancy was relatively low. Both blacks and whites who survived to adulthood could live to well beyond the age of thirty.

MUSCLE ATTACHMENTS

Closer study of the bones revealed marks called lesions, found where muscles had been attached to bones. Lesions indicated the muscles were large and defined. These details proved the slaves had done hard physical labor, probably daily. The lesions also showed the muscles had torn, then healed, and then torn again due to this hard work. Because the lesion scars on the oldest individuals had

Arthritis caused the protrusions on the bones shown here. Years of heavy lifting, pulling, pounding, and plowing caused this condition in the Schuyler farm slaves.

not healed, Anderson concluded they "continued to work hard up until the day they died." She also suspected the slaves did heavy farmwork and housework. The lesions and the wear on bones in the backs and upper bodies indicated the slaves performed jobs that required the same movements over and over again. These would have been activities such as lifting, hoeing, and pounding. As a result of the daily and lifelong strain, all the adults had developed arthritis, a condition in which joints become inflamed and painful.

Some adults showed signs of having had anemia, a blood condition that can cause extreme fatigue. But these cases had all been mild and well-healed. There was no evidence for anemia on the bones of the three children complete enough to study. Swelling of joints on adult fingers came from spinning thread, weaving, and other manual jobs. The oldest woman had four broken ribs, perhaps the result of a fall. The ribs had been healing, so her death wasn't caused by their breaking. Anderson and Dale speculated she could have died from a disease, such as pneumonia, or from heart failure.

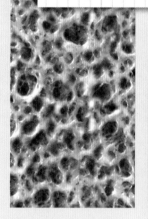
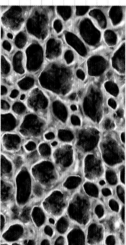

Bone analysis also includes the texture of bones. Spongy bones, such as the one at right, indicate a poor diet.

The archaeologists also checked to see if the bones were spongy. Bones become spongy as a result of poor diet, one that lacks a combination of meat, vegetables, and fruit. These skeletons' bones weren't spongy. Anderson concluded the slaves "found ways to procure adequate nutrition, whether by raising kitchen gardens and livestock of their own or harvesting plants and animals from the wild."

TEETH

Most of the skeletons had bad teeth. This was not unusual. People in the 1700s didn't take care of their teeth the way people do now. Even George Washington had only one tooth left when he became president. When disease or nutritional distress occurs, lines form on teeth. Four adults and one child had lines, which indicated they had suffered from malnutrition at some point. The lines were very faint and thin, suggesting a mild or brief stress event in childhood. More than half of the skeletons from the Schuyler farm adult burials had cavities, infected gums, and missing teeth. The oldest woman had no teeth at all. Each tooth that falls out leaves a hole in the jaw. The holes in the oldest woman's jaw had completely healed over and disappeared. Her teeth had been gone for many years.

In this era, wealthy white people who lost their teeth often could afford to have false teeth made. That wouldn't have been an option for a slave. The toothless woman would have had to gum her food. Those with cavities would have chewed their food with difficulty and pain.

Two little dips worn into some of the man's upper and lower teeth suggested he smoked a pipe. Cigarettes and cigars didn't exist yet, so smokers used white clay tobacco pipes. The wear on his teeth showed he held the pipe stem tightly on the left side of his mouth. Some women in the 1700s also smoked pipes, though the practice wasn't common. Two women from the burial site had this same kind of wear marks on their teeth.

Another female had a groove in one of her lower teeth. The groove was probably made by

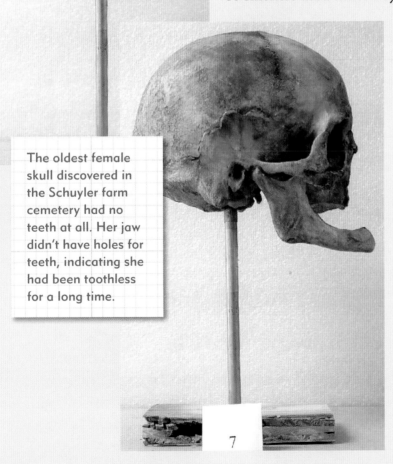

The oldest female skull discovered in the Schuyler farm cemetery had no teeth at all. Her jaw didn't have holes for teeth, indicating she had been toothless for a long time.

7

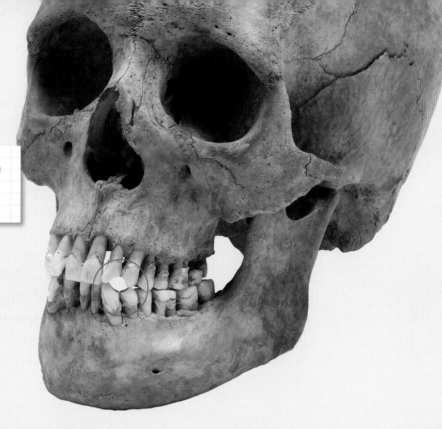

A groove in several teeth indicated that a person was a pipe smoker.

pulling thread across the tooth for years. From this small clue, the archaeologists concluded one of her jobs was to sew for the Schuyler family and for her own family.

Teeth store chemical traces called isotopes from food and water. Different areas of the world have different food and water. By studying the isotopes in teeth, scientists can tell where people once lived. Anderson knew many slaves brought to New York from Africa spent time working on plantations in the Caribbean or were born there. An expert on teeth from Caribbean burials studied the Schuyler slaves' teeth. She found no similarities to the teeth of people who had lived in the Caribbean at this time, so Anderson could conclude that none of these slaves had ever lived in the Caribbean. All the people excavated from the Schuyler farm cemetery had been born in the United States.

DNA STUDIES

After learning all they could from the bones and teeth, the state museum scientists were ready to examine the skeletons' deoxyribonucleic acid (DNA) for more clues. The researchers extracted DNA samples from the seven adult skeletons.

Four adults in this burial ground were related to African Americans who came from West or West-Central Africa. They were clearly of African descent. One of these four adults, a woman, also had American Indian ancestry. One of her female ancestors must have been American Indian. Her DNA matched that

How DNA Is Sampled

DNA stands for deoxyribonucleic acid. It is in nearly every one of our cells and can be found in bones. Study of DNA can reveal information about a person's ancestors. One particular segment of DNA passes unbroken through the female line. A scientist can use this to work out connections between daughters, mothers, grandmothers, great-grandmothers, and so on. Determining the male line through DNA is much more difficult. The science is not yet fully developed.

Many DNA samples are drilled from a bone. The samples are then put in sterile test tubes. Various chemicals are added, and each tube is heated and shaken until a final filtered sample is obtained. Such samples can be compared to others. The female ancestry of the individual is then determined.

The white material in the test tube is DNA.

of the Micmac Indians of eastern Canada. Anderson concluded the woman's father's ancestors must have been African. American Indian DNA along with African DNA had been found before, but the combination was not typical for the area.

The DNA of two other women showed different ancestry. They were descendants of women who lived on the island of Madagascar, located off the eastern coast of Africa. Trade with Madagascar in the 1700s was officially forbidden, but historical research shows New York merchants traded there anyway. Pirates in the Madagascar area sold Africans captured on that island at a cheap price. These two women probably had ancestors whom pirates had captured and sold into slavery.

The DNA showed that all the adults had different mothers, so none were related to the others through the female line. DNA couldn't be derived from the children's bones, but it's very likely they were related to the women from the cemetery.

The slaves were of very diverse origins—West African, North American, and Madagascan. Because the archaeologists had first thought the slaves were only of African descent, this finding about the history of slaves was important. While the slaves had all worked on the same farm, it was becoming clear they came from a variety of backgrounds. The stories of how they came to live on this farm were all distinct.

MORE RESEARCH

To learn even more about the lives of the slaves on Schuyler farm, the state museum scientists turned to a book written by someone who had lived there. Anne Grant had spent part of her childhood at the Schuyler farm in the 1750s and 1760s. She was the daughter of a British soldier. While her father was away on duty, Mrs. Schuyler invited the child to stay with her.

Grant later wrote a book about her life at the farm. She described the slaves she knew. She said the two oldest women, Diana and Maria, had come from Africa when they were very young. One white-haired man, whom she didn't name, sat by the chimney making shoes. Prince cut wood. Caesar cut and threshed wheat. Betty sewed and did laundry. Rachel cooked. Other slaves made cider, raised hemp and tobacco, fished, and tended horses, including shoeing them. The slaves also made nets and did carpentry, including making canoes and paddles.

Grant wrote that punishment of slaves was rare, except "when a member showed symptoms of degeneracy [not behaving as he/she should], he was immediately expelled or in other words, sold." She noticed that "each family [she] knew had few [slaves]." Slaves were born and lived in the same house as their enslavers. As a result, there was "little or no difference with regard to food or clothing between their children and those of their master." And the Schuyler farm slaves tended little gardens where "they raised herbs or plants of difficult culture."

> Grant wrote that punishment of slaves was rare, except "when a member showed symptoms of degeneracy [not behaving as he/she should], he was immediately expelled or in other words, sold."

Analysis of the bones supported Grant's description of the slaves' lives. They had been well fed. They worked very hard. While the information Grant provided was interesting, her story of her life at Schuyler farm had to be used carefully. She lived at the farm as a child and wrote the book as an adult, so her recollections may have been inexact. But her account is useful because the findings from the bone analysis support her statements about the lives of the slaves there.

THE SCHUYLER FARM BONES

All the information the New York State Museum scientists gathered about the Schuyler farm bones—the forgotten bones—is important. It helps create an understanding of the lives of slaves who lived and died on the farm. Early deaths, hard work, ancestry, arthritis, and fractures: the bones revealed many details.

In her study findings, in addition to noting what she had learned, Anderson also reminded readers of an important aspect of social history. She wrote, "A 'lifetime of hard work' meant laboring to support the households that enslaved them and enhance the prosperity of their owners." She also added that slaves lived with "forced labor, infant deaths, and the lack of freedom to make choices for one's self and one's family except perhaps in death."

CHAPTER THREE

RECONSTRUCTING FACES

Gay Malin, a facial reconstructionist, sat quietly studying the seven skulls in front of her. One was a male, and the others were females ages thirty to sixty. The subjects came from those found at the Schuyler farm burial grounds and were complete enough for her to attempt reconstructing their faces, a process that combines art and science. Malin didn't rush. She wanted to do it right.

Anderson had provided the skulls along with information about each. Malin read through the facts: their ages, their sex, and their ancestry. These details would help her work out how the faces might have looked.

Next, she studied the bones in each skull to see how robust each person was. Bone size is an important clue to facial appearances. Slender bones suggest a smaller, petite face. Large bones suggest the opposite.

Satisfied with her study, Malin sealed in eye sockets, noses, and other openings in the skulls with clay. Then she poured silicon rubber around each skull. She did this in three sections for the head and in two sections for the jaw. Then she removed the rubber. She set aside the original skulls to be reunited with their respective skeletons.

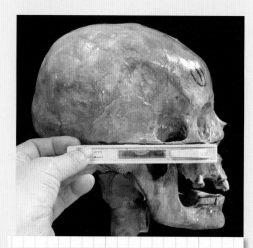

Malin carefully measured the facial bones to help create accurate reconstructions.

Now Malin had pieces to create a rubber mold of each skull. After fastening the sections of each rubber mold together, she poured a liquid plastic into them to cast the faces. The plastic hardened, making exact replicas of the skulls. She did this twice for each skull. She would leave one of each for further study as she proceeded to work with the second one.

Malin used information gathered by various scientists to decide how thick the skin and flesh tissue on slave faces would have been. After putting some clay onto the replica skull, she pushed in white plastic markers to show the proper skin depths. Then she added clay strips and sculpted them to represent the larger muscles on the face. She used still more clay for glands and chins. Malin spread a thin layer for skin and textured it using deer skin, which she had discovered closely resembles the texture of human

Blending Art and Science

Gay Malin received her college degree in fine arts, majoring in sculpture. While a student, she won a national art competition. Malin has worked at the New York State Museum for more than twenty years as a specialist in conserving historic objects and creating special exhibits. She has restored and conserved several mastodons and made human figures for dioramas. When archaeologists at the museum began finding skeletons during their projects, Malin was happy to use her artistic and scientific knowledge to reconstruct the faces of these long-forgotten individuals. As a result of her work, Malin has become recognized as a specialist in the field of facial reconstruction.

Malin made plastic molds of each skull to serve as the foundation of her reconstructions. That way, the real skulls could be preserved and returned to their respective skeletons.

skin. For many of her other facial restoration projects, Malin consulted with hair historians and historic paintings to choose the proper wig style for the period when the person was alive. This time, however, she decided to take on the difficult task of making hair out of clay. Malin pressed fistfuls of fine wire into clay to make some curly hair. Because American Indian women usually did not cut their hair, she rolled clay together in tendrils to replicate the long hair of the woman with African American and American Indian ancestry.

Malin's next step was making a new rubber mold of the fully sculpted face. Pouring white plaster into these second molds produced a hard version of the faces. The clay sculptures were destroyed during this process, but she still had the original rubber mold of the skulls set aside in case she needed to start over.

Malin hand-painted the plaster faces. She varied the skin tone to represent the color it may have been, with some people having lighter brown skin and others having darker brown. The shades of the slaves' skin would have varied in the same way the shades of white people's do. She painted the older woman's hair a mixture of gray and white. She painted the hair of the rest of the replicas black.

After painting, Malin added a wash that prevents light from reflecting off the faces. The effect mimics human skin, which absorbs light. Finally, she added glass eyes.

Malin's hours and hours of work and artistry allow people to glimpse the faces of slaves from an eighteenth-century northern cemetery for the first and, so far, only time. The bones from Schuyler farm were part of living, breathing people. Malin's work has brought the bones to life for museum visitors.

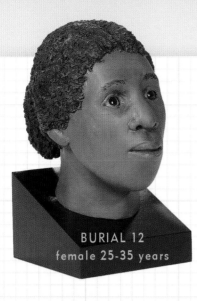

BURIAL 12
female 25-35 years

Malin's facial reconstructions combine both art and science to bring to life the people buried in the cemetery. Each reconstruction gives a glimpse into the face of a person who once walked the acres of the Schuyler farm.

BURIAL 15
male 40-50 years

BURIAL 3
female 30-40 years

BURIAL 13
female 30-40 years

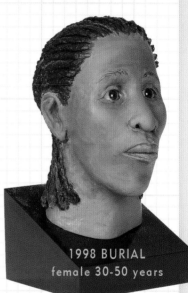

1998 BURIAL
female 30-50 years

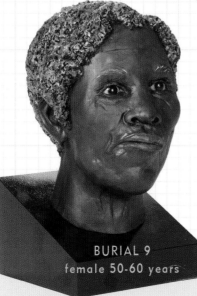

BURIAL 9
female 50-60 years

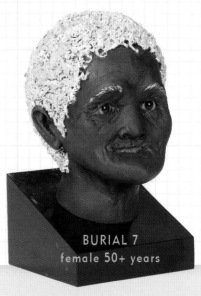

BURIAL 7
female 50+ years

CHAPTER FOUR

NORTHERN CEMETERIES

Completing the excavations, bone studies, and facial reconstructions answered many questions, but the archaeologists working on the Schuyler farm project faced more questions. How closely did the bones of the Schuyler farm slaves compare with those found in the two other northern burial grounds? Were the origins, illnesses, injuries, and ages at death of the Schuyler farm slaves the same as those from these other cemeteries, or were the lives of the African Americans at the Schuyler farm unique?

Researchers would look into these very questions. By comparing information about the skeletons found at the different sites, they hoped to find the answers.

BURIAL GROUNDS

In Portsmouth, New Hampshire, scientists found slave burials as deep as 8 feet (2.4 meters) underground and as shallow as 2 feet (0.6 m). In New York City, though, the burial ground had been covered over many times throughout the years. By the time the cemetery was discovered, the burials lay 17 feet (5 m) to 24 feet (7 m) belowground.

Ground surfaces in cities build up rapidly due to constant human activity. Earlier surfaces become covered over and forgotten. The Schuyler farm burials were discovered approximately 2 feet (0.6 m) down, among the shallowest discoveries of all three sites.

CHILDREN

In all three cemeteries, half of the burials were children. The deaths of so many children brought the average age at death for all the burials to approximately

SLAVE CEMETERIES IN THE NORTH

Portsmouth, NH•

Albany, NY•

New York, NY•

twenty-two. A white cemetery at Schuyler farm sat near the house. The archaeologists gathered information from the inscriptions on the stones. Sixteen white people had died in the late 1700s and early 1800s. Only three were infants, making up 18 percent of the deaths, which was much lower than the 50 percent represented in the slave burials. Two hundred of the more than four hundred burials found in New York City were children, and half of those were infants. Child mortality was higher for slaves than for white children.

Slave women didn't receive good care while they were pregnant, including not having access to a doctor in an emergency the way white mothers might have. Slave women continued difficult physical work throughout their pregnancies. After giving birth, they quickly returned to doing difficult tasks. Because of these differences, the babies of the enslaved were probably born weaker and had less healthy infancies. Slave children were also susceptible to diseases such as smallpox, yellow fever, and measles, without the care and attention most white children would have received.

COFFINS

In all three burial grounds, most of the coffins were six-cornered and built from eastern white pine. At Schuyler farm, the coffins were buried in rows and at a common depth. But in the two city burial grounds, coffins had sometimes been placed on top of one another.

In Portsmouth, one surprise for the researchers was how carefully the coffins had been placed in the ground. Gravediggers in the 1700s had cut down through the earth all the way into the hard bedrock. They had clearly wanted the coffins to lay flat so their loved ones, even in death, would rest undisturbed by the settling of the soil.

One coffin had partly collapsed down into the one below it. The upper coffin contained the remains of a child who had died between the ages of seven and eleven. The child may have been related to the man aged twenty-one to forty in the coffin below. Or perhaps the cemetery had become so overcrowded that new burials had to be placed over the top of older ones.

In New York, archaeologists often found coffins on top of others. The archaeologists understood why when they found some graves marked with standing stones or outlined with cobblestones.

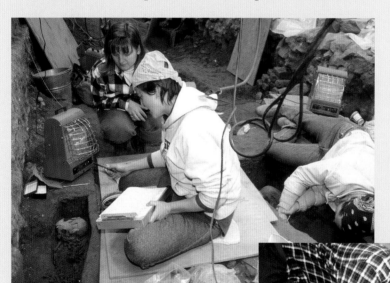

Archaeologists in New York City excavated some of the bones at a large slave cemetery discovered in 1991.

This suggested families knew which burial plots were theirs. They buried their relatives together, sometimes placing new over old. Where stone markers weren't found, wood posts and boards probably had been placed to mark the graves, but they had deteriorated long ago. Archaeologists from the Schuyler farm project and the Portsmouth project believe wood markers also once stood in those cemeteries. The burial grounds in the cities had probably become very crowded, unlike the Schuyler farm cemetery, which had much more land available—and many fewer slaves.

THE BONES

The Portsmouth and New York City bones also had been buried in areas separate from white cemeteries. All the bones belonged to African Americans. Researchers discovered lesions on the bones, just as Anderson and Dale had discovered lesions on the bones from Schuyler farm. These stress marks showed that muscles tore, healed, and tore again, especially in chests and shoulders. Both adults and children had strained their muscles stooping over to lift and pull heavy objects over and over again.

These freed slaves are picking peanuts in Virginia in the late 1890s. Even after slavery ended in the United States, hard physical labor was a reality for many black families.

In New York City, the bones of the slaves also bore marks left by illnesses and disorders, such as tuberculosis, a highly contagious disease that affects the lungs. Disease spread more quickly among people crowded together in cities. Rickets was also a problem. The disorder results from malnutrition. Many pitted, spongy bones from the New York City site indicated malnutrition. Research of New York City historical records shows that a slave's meals consisted mostly of cornmeal and very little meat. Corn is not very nutritious, but milk is, so it was added to the cornmeal. However, many African Americans could not easily digest cow's milk or the cheese made from it. Even in the twenty-first century, intolerance to the enzymes in dairy products is quite common worldwide. But people of European ancestry, such as the white farm owners who would have owned slaves in the 1700s, have developed a genetic mutation that makes drinking milk and eating cheese tolerable. The slaves would not have had this mutation, so dairy products would have made most of them quite sick. Their bodies couldn't absorb calcium and protein from these foods either. This resulted in a spongy bone texture, which was not found in the Schuyler farm bones.

The Portsmouth bones were damaged by sewage and water seeping into the cemetery. Archaeologists couldn't determine whether the slaves buried there had been sick or malnourished.

TEETH

In both the Portsmouth and New York City sites, some of the skulls had modified teeth. The teeth had been deliberately chipped and filed into different shapes, such as pegs, hourglasses, or points.

The filed tooth *(third from right)* told researchers that the person probably lived in Africa until at least the age of thirteen.

In some West African tribes, children were considered adults after an initiation at about the age of thirteen. Part of the rite of passage included pulling lower teeth and filing upper ones into different shapes. Slave children born in America often didn't go through such an initiation. The researchers theorized the people with modified teeth had probably lived in Africa until they were teenagers. After the age of thirteen, they had been captured and sold into slavery. No such treatment of teeth was found at the Schuyler farm burial site. The absence of teeth modifications was further evidence the slaves buried there hadn't been born in Africa.

Most of the people found at all three burial sites were missing teeth and had cavities and gum infections. Tooth and mouth pain would have been common. Chewing certain foods would have been excruciating.

Scientists also found grooves in some of the New York City teeth that had developed during times when the slaves weren't eating well. Getting enough food, let alone wholesome food, was a serious problem for slaves in this city. The grooves were especially common on the teeth of children who had died before the age of fifteen. But the teeth from the young slaves showed there were times in their lives when they didn't have food. They didn't starve to death, but the times when they didn't have enough food would have damaged their health and made them so weak their bodies wouldn't have been able to fight off disease.

Researchers in New York City tested the teeth from the slaves buried there to see what isotopes were present. They learned slaves had eaten foods unique to West and West-Central Africa. The researchers could confirm their original theory. The isotopes and modifications to the teeth proved those slaves in New York City had been born in Africa. Because the teeth in the Schuyler farm burials weren't modified and didn't contain isotopes from elsewhere, the scientists could conclude that the Schuyler farm's slaves had been born in the United States.

> They didn't starve to death, but the times when they didn't have enough food would have damaged their health and made them so weak their bodies wouldn't have been able to fight off disease.

DNA STUDIES

DNA of the bones from all three sites showed most of the slaves either came directly from or were descended from relatives born in West Africa, including places now referred to as Congo, Ghana, and Benin. As with the Schuyler farm bones, DNA tests showed Madagascan ancestry in some of the New York City graves. This fact and the carved teeth suggested that they had been acquired illegally from pirates. Tribal warfare and trade competition in Africa led to the capture of many people by their rivals. Captors marched their captives to the coast for sale to slave traders, who purchased them, loaded them on ships, and took them to Europe, the Caribbean, and the Americas.

African slaves who came to the United States brought many of their customs, languages, and beliefs with them. Once they were sold, slaves had to adjust to new customs, languages and, for many, a new religion—Christianity. Many slaves taught or continued to teach their children African beliefs and customs. Several generations passed before Christianity fully replaced beliefs in gods who resided in rivers, trees, and rocks. The belief that the spirits of their ancestors continued to influence their lives was especially strong among African slaves. Ceremonies to placate these spirits were central to their religions. West Africans honored their dead loved ones with burials that included singing, drumming, bell ringing, and dancing. The enslaved carried on these customs as much as possible in America. In 1865 a New York City clerk wrote that New Yorkers still remembered and talked about the African American burial ground there. He said many of the Africans "retained their burial customs, among which was that of burying with various mummeries and outcries."

Many white people considered the slaves' celebration of their dead ancestors blasphemous, or non-Christian. Whites eventually outlawed slave funeral parades in Boston, Massachusetts, and limited the number of participants in New York City parades. The slave owners on the Caribbean Island of Saint Kitts even prohibited drumming. Forbidding slaves from their religious practices and banning large assemblies was one way owners tried to control slaves and to prevent revolts.

UNIQUE FINDS

The burial grounds in New York City were large and contained at least one thousand slave bodies. The cemetery had been used for more than one hundred

years, so it held many more people than the other two, smaller cemeteries. Archaeologists excavated more than four hundred bodies from the New York City site. The burial grounds held more remains, but they were left undisturbed after

Forbidding slaves from their religious practices and banning large assemblies was one way owners tried to control slaves and to prevent revolts.

a construction project that had been in progress was redesigned to protect the rest of the graves. For the researchers studying the cemetery, the large number of recovered burials provided unique and important information not seen in the smaller samples from Schuyler farm and at Portsmouth.

In the New York City cemetery, for example, loved ones had left gifts with the dead in eighty graves, which proved that African practices still existed there. In one man's grave, researchers discovered a cluster of small metal rings and a line of pins along his arm bone. The pins had once fastened a small cloth bundle that had rotted away. Researchers speculated slaves believed the rings contained magic the man's spirit could use after death. Belief in conjuring bags, as they were known to the slaves, came from Africa. The gift suggested the man had been a spiritual leader among his people. Archaeologists have found similar bundles in the graves of slaves buried in southern states, as well as in the Caribbean Islands.

The heart shape on the lid of this coffin discovered in the New York City cemetery is called the Sankofa. It suggests slaves in the Americas maintained a connection to the symbols that had meaning in West Africa.

On top of another coffin, researchers discovered a heart-shaped design made with nails and tacks. It is the *Sankofa*, a symbol from Ghana and the Ivory Coast in the 1700s that translates to mean roughly "learn from the past to prepare for the future." To slaves in America, this was a symbol of endurance.

In another case, a string of 112 blue, green, and white beads and some shells remained around a woman's waist. The woman had modified teeth, which indicated she had been born in Africa. The colors of the beads are significant. Some slaves believed the colors of the beads represented water. The beads would perhaps help her spirit cross the ocean back to her family in Africa. Altogether the presence of the conjuring bundles, the Sankofa, and the beads suggest that some slaves in New York City still felt connected to the customs and traditions of West Africa.

BONES

Twenty-three males and eighteen females in the New York City cemetery had suffered broken bones that probably contributed to their deaths. Skull fractures, in particular, were common. The slaves had been beaten on the head with an object and had died from the injuries. Through careful study, researchers speculated that one woman had been killed while trying to run away. In addition to having a broken arm, possibly from being grabbed, she had a bullet hole in her back and mutilated face bones, likely the result of being hit with the butt of a gun. New bone growth in her face suggested she lived at least a few days before dying. She was approximately twenty years old. Slaves often suffered severe physical punishment for disobeying their masters. No laws existed to protect slaves from brutal treatment. Evidence of severe abuse was not found in the other two burial grounds, but harsh treatment such as whippings, which were common at the time, do not leave marks on a skeleton's bones and can't be scientifically confirmed.

The Threat of Being Sold

One of a slave's biggest fears was being sold. An advertisement in New York City's *Daily Advertiser* for June 8, 1793, proclaimed, **"To be sold: a black family consisting of a man, his wife, a fine girl about twelve, another girl about five years old, and a male child. It is a useful trustworthy comely family, and of late years accustomed to live in this city. The above will be sold either separate or altogether."**

CHAPTER FIVE

NORTHERN SLAVE LIFE

The bones, teeth, and gifts left with slaves buried in the Schuyler farm, Portsmouth, and New York City cemeteries reveal much about slaves' lives. It's possible to learn where the enslaved came from, their gender, age, and ancestry. Sometimes researchers can even determine the cause of death. Documents such as newspapers, posters, and journals help modern researchers put together the story of the bones. Together the bones and the documentation create a more complete picture of a slave's life than either resource would do alone.

SLAVE RESISTANCE

Slaves owners typically viewed slaves as troublesome children. As early as 1659, a Dutchman reported his slave was "too proud." The Dutchman said the slave's manner was such that "it's bad enough here to get him to do [duties] so that at times I have to punish him."

In another example, a letter written by a storekeeper notes a slave in 1710 stole money and was whipped. And in a 1717 letter, the writer recorded that a female slave showed "growing independence of mind," lied frequently, and was sullen, so she was sold. Another slave-owning family described its slaves as "unruly, disobedient, wicked," causing the family to feel they were "slave to the slaves." And another northern family felt a father and daughter slave family caused unwelcome trouble in 1799. The slave father crept out at night

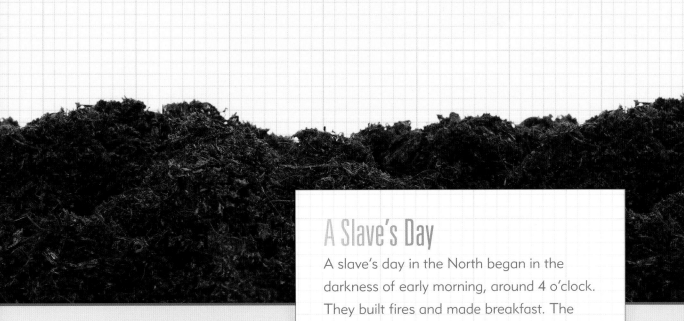

at the invitation of white neighbors and played his fiddle for parties in their houses. The owner couldn't control this slave, so he threatened to sue his neighbors for encouraging the slave to disobey him. The slave's daughter was described as having "unbridled attitude" and a "lack of docility."

Slave resistance took many forms. Some slaves broke tools, talked back, dragged their feet, or pretended to be sick. These actions gave them at least some control over their lives. At times, slaves revolted violently. And some escaped.

A Slave's Day

A slave's day in the North began in the darkness of early morning, around 4 o'clock. They built fires and made breakfast. The enslavers could then sit down to enjoy a meal by the warmth of a fire. Slave children worked alongside their parents and were put to work when they were as young as two. Slave children swept floors, cleaned rooms, ran errands, fetched water, sewed, and cared for younger children. From an early age, they lifted heavy objects such as cooking pots. Adults worked in the fields, cleaned the house, washed laundry, and sewed. At the end of a long day, they waited for their enslavers to go to bed before banking down fireplace fires, cleaning up any messes, and securing the doors. Only then could they go to sleep in the kitchen, the cellar, or the attic. In a few hours, they would get up and start it all again. Even in death, slaves were controlled. White owners chose the locations for slave cemeteries, usually far from where whites lived and buried their own dead. White cemeteries were preserved over time. Slave cemeteries were forgotten.

Revolt?

In March 1741, in New York City, a fire occurred in the fort where government officials were housed. People rushed in to keep it from spreading to nearby houses. Rain that night ended the emergency. But everyone wondered how it had started. Eight days later, fire broke out near the area. A few days after that, a warehouse caught fire and spread to other buildings. Four days after that, a stable burned. And a fire broke out at a house nearby. It seemed that a straw mattress in the attic had been lit. Fear spread when four more fires started the next day.

White New Yorkers were convinced slaves were setting the fires. Mobs of white people took to the streets and eventually rounded up almost every black male older than fifteen. A judge met with the city's leaders. Together they determined that sixty-two black men were to be executed for the fires. Others were sent into slavery elsewhere. Some were returned to their owners.

Were the condemned men all responsible for the fires? Some did confess to committing arson out of anger for the way they were treated. But the number of men involved in the fires remains a mystery.

A crowd watches a black man being burned alive in New York City in 1741. Such public killings were meant to discourage other slaves from rebelling.

SHORTER LIVES

Slaves in the North did not live as long as white northerners around them. All eight adults studied in Portsmouth died in their thirties. At the Schuyler farm and New York City burial grounds, few bones belonged to elderly people. White cemeteries of the same period also show many young people died. But many others lived to an older age, probably because they ate better, had better living conditions, and got more rest than slaves. Some historians say whites were five times more likely than slaves to survive past the age of fifty-five.

Some historians say whites were five times more likely than slaves to survive past the age of fifty-five.

FORMING COMMUNITIES

In the South, hundreds of slaves lived together in wooden cabins away from the main house, where the slave owner lived. These slave communities overcame differences in languages and customs. They worked in the fields together, married, raised children, and buried their dead. Some southern slaves lived and worked in the main house, and they formed their own communities separate from those of the field slaves.

In the North, most slaves didn't have a broad community for support. Typically only one or two slaves lived and worked in a northern household. As a result, slaves in the North were more isolated. Some northern slaves, however, were able to form communities in areas with larger slave populations, a fact proven in burial practices. Archaeologists in New York City discovered that individuals who came directly from Africa were buried in the same areas as those who were born in the Americas. There was no separation. Researchers believe this shows the slaves were part of one community. In addition, shared graves and groups buried close together suggest close ties, either of friendship or family. In one case, a forty-year-old man and a thirty-year-old woman lay side by side in identical coffins. Their ages and the proximity of their remains suggest a connection based on family, friendship, or love. Historical records show that other slaves adopted children who were orphaned when their parents were sold. And church records indicate slaves witnessed one another's weddings and were godparents for one another's children.

PUTTING A FACE ON HISTORY

All three slave cemeteries were excavated with care and respect by archaeologists who were supported by local governments and communities. In New York City, the bones of the slaves were reburied at a public ceremony attended by the mayor and other guests. The National Park Service built a large memorial and a museum to tell the story of slavery in the city.

In Portsmouth, plans are being developed for a memorial there. In the meantime, signs on the street at the burial grounds tell the story of their discovery. More remains lie under the street. City officials have pledged to keep them safe and undisturbed.

More burials may exist at Schuyler farm too. Further investigations are planned using

We remember the men and women who built Portsmouth and the hardships they bore in free, indentured or enslaved labor. This burying ground was a segregated space and its story is a verified and tangible piece of Portsmouth's early 18th century history.

African Burying Ground
Future Memorial Park
www.AfricanBuryingGroundNH.org

Ceremonies, information placards, and museums all contribute to awareness of slavery's legacy in the North.

African Burial Ground National Monument
National Park Service
U.S. Department of the Interior

ground-penetrating radar. This system beams radio waves into the ground. If the waves hit a solid object, such as a coffin, they bounce back. This method could determine the size of the entire cemetery without disturbing its contents. Meanwhile, Anderson has safely stored the bones from Schuyler farm at the state museum. She is also preparing a more detailed report on their analysis. Reburial of the bones of the slaves lies in the future.

Of the three sites, reconstruction of faces has occurred only with the Schuyler farm individuals. The archaeologists who worked on the Schuyler farm project did more than find bones in the ground. They discovered people, and the faces Malin created from the skulls make this very clear. Malin's work will be part of a special exhibit at the New York State Museum that will also include the story of the burial discovery and information about the lives of slaves at the Schuyler farm. More than two centuries after they lived and died, these forgotten people are being remembered and treated with respect.

AUTHOR'S NOTE

As an archaeologist in upstate New York, I was fortunate enough to visit the excavations at Schuyler farm and became interested in learning more about slavery in the North. I interviewed archaeologists, historians, members of the local black community, and bioarchaeologists who worked on skeletons from all three burial grounds. All of these experts were generous with their knowledge and time and very helpful. I am grateful to them all for helping to open my eyes to life for people enslaved in the North.

My husband and I spent time in Portsmouth, New Hampshire, visiting the burial site there and doing research at the city library. We also took the train to New York City to study the exhibits and the outdoor memorial at the African American Burial Ground site. Both are powerful and fascinating.

I found that I knew more about slavery in the South than in the North. Yet in both regions, slaves received little credit for their contributions to the growth of the United States. They did that work in fear of being sold and separated from their families and under threat of being punished for any little thing. White society set slaves apart as inferior beings—in life and in death.

These three burial grounds were on their way to being destroyed. I am very moved that they are being rescued by archaeologists. These bones can play a vital role in helping us to better understand the lives of enslaved people in the North and their contributions to our nation.

GLOSSARY

acid-free tissue paper: tissue paper that does not corrode the items it touches. Archaeologists use it to protect bones and other objects.

analysis: careful study of something to learn about its parts and its meaning

ancestry: a person's biological, family roots

anemia: a condition in which a person has fewer red blood cells than normal and feels very weak and tired

arthritis: a condition that causes a person's joints to become swollen and painful

artifact: an object made or used by people in the past

bank down: cover a fire with ashes to help it go out safely

bioarchaeologist: a scientist who studies human remains from the past

Caribbean: relating to the Caribbean Sea (which is an arm of the Atlantic Ocean), the islands in that region, or the people who live there

cavity: a hole in a tooth caused by decay

comely: pretty or attractive

conserve: to keep something from being destroyed or damaged

deteriorate: to wear away over time

deoxyribonucleic acid (DNA): a chemical carrying all genetic information. DNA is found in the nucleus of nearly all cells in plants and animals.

diorama: a small model of someone or something, usually in 3-D perspective

enzyme: a chemical substance in the cells of living things that helps with processes, such as digesting food

era: a specific period of time in history

excavate: to uncover something by removing the soil or debris on top of it

expel: to drive away someone or something by force

expertise: special skills or knowledge

filter screen: a tool used by archaeologists to help sift through piles of dirt to separate larger items from the soil

fracture: a crack or break in a bone

genetic: relating to genes, the segments of DNA that influence something's appearance, growth, and other traits

gland: an organ in the body that makes substances that can be used by other parts of the body

hunch: a belief or feeling about something that is not based on facts

integral: important or essential

isotope: a specific chemical form of atom. Isotopes in teeth can reveal where a person lived.

lesion: an injured spot on a person's body

mourner: a person who grieves the loss of someone who has died

mummers: people who make noises as part of a funeral

mutation: a random, accidental change in one or more genes

mutilate: to severely damage or destroy

nasal cavities: the air-filled space above and behind the nose

plantation: a large piece of land where slaves raised crops such as cotton and rice in the American South

pneumonia: a disease of the lungs

reconstruct: to rebuild something that is broken or destroyed

rickets: a disease found in animals and young people who don't get enough vitamin D

scale drawing: a drawing on paper that shows an object's actual size in relation to its surroundings

shroud: a cloth used to wrap a body before burial

sue: when a person or group of people use the law to try and get another person or group to pay them or do something for them

speculate: to make a guess about something, especially without knowing all the facts

sullen: sad, unhappy

taxing: difficult

tendril: a thin and curly piece of fiber or other material

trowel: a tool archaeologists use to gently scrape soil off artifacts

tuberculosis: a disease of the lungs that can also affect other parts of the body

SOURCE NOTES

4   Kevin Franklin, interview with the author, June 5, 2013.

13 Matthew Kirk, interview with the author, April 23, 2013.

17 Corey McQuinn, interview with the author, April 23, 2013.

20 Lisa Anderson, interview with the author, June 5, 2013.

20 Lisa Anderson, "Proposed Bioarchaeological Analysis of Human Remains from Route 32, Menands, NY," New York State Historical Preservation Office, June 2005.

24 Lisa Anderson, Vanessa Dale, and Dawn M. Lawrence, "Life, Work, and Death among the 18th Century African Americans in Rural Upstate New York," presentation to the Northeast Anthropological Association, Albany, NY, May 2006.

24 Ibid.

28 Anne Grant, *Memoirs of an American Lady* (Albany, NY: Joel Munsell, 1876), 179.

28 Ibid., 51.

28 Ibid.

28 Ibid., 182.

29 Anderson, Dale, and Lawrence, "Life, Work."

40 Anne-Marie Cantwell and Diana diZerega Wall, *Unearthing Gotham: The Archaeology of New York City* (New Haven, CT: Yale University, 2001), 279.

43 *Daily Advertiser* (New York, NY), June 8, 1793, 4.

44 A.J.F. Van Laer, *Correspondence of Jeremias van Rensselaer 1651–1674*, (Albany, NY: The University of the State of New York, 1932), 167.

44 Cadwallader Colden, *The Letters and Papers of Cadwallader Colden, 1711–1729*, vol. 1, (New York: Printed for the New York Historical Society, 1918), 39.

44 Ibid., 157.

45 Jacob Judd, ed., *Correspondence of the Van Cortlandt Family of Cortlandt Manor 1748–1800*, vol. 2, (Tarrytown, NY: Sleepy Hollow Restorations, 1977), 595.

LERNER

SOURCE

Expand learning beyond the printed book. Download free, complementary educational resources for this book from our website, www.lerneresource.com.

SELECTED BIBLIOGRAPHY

Anderson, Lisa M. "Proposed Bioarchaeological Analysis of Human Remains from Route 32, Menands, NY." Research Proposal, Historic Preservation Office, June 2005.

Grant, Anne. *Memoirs of an American Lady.* Albany, NY: Joel Munsell, 1876.

Lee, Esther J., Lisa M. Anderson, Vanessa Dale, D. Andrew Merriwether. "MtDNA Origins of an Enslaved Labor Force from the 18th century Schuyler Flatts Burial Ground in Colonial Albany, NY: Africans, Native Americans, and Malagasy?" *Journal of Archaeological Science* 36, no. 12 (December 2009): 2805–2810.

The New York African Burial Ground: Unearthing the African Presence in Colonial New York, vols. 1–4. United States General Services Administration (GSA), 2009. Washington, DC: Howard University Press, 2009. CD-ROM.

Walker, Sally M. *Their Skeletons Speak: Kennewick Man and the Paleoamerican World.* Minneapolis: Carolrhoda Books, 2012.

FOR MORE INFORMATION

BOOKS

Deem, James M. *Faces from the Past: Forgotten People of North America.* Boston: Houghton Mifflin Harcourt, 2012.

Goodson, Martia G. *New York's African Burial Ground.* Fort Washington, PA: Eastern National Parks, 2012.

Huey, Lois Miner. *American Archaeology Uncovers the Underground Railroad.* Tarrytown, NY: Marshall Cavendish Benchmark, 2010.

MacLeod, Elizabeth. *Bones Never Lie: How Forensics Helps Solve History's Mysteries.* Toronto: Annick Press, 2013.

Walker, Sally M. *Written in Bone: Buried Lives of Jamestown and Colonial Maryland.* Minneapolis: Carolrhoda Books, 2009.

WEBSITES

Born in Slavery: Slave Narratives from the Federal Writers' Project, 1936–1938
http://lcweb2.loc.gov/ammem/snhtml/snhome.html
This site contains more than twenty-three hundred accounts of slavery, given during the 1930s by people who had lived as slaves. Viewers can search the accounts by keyword or browse by the names of states or the names of the former slaves.

Discovery School: Understanding Slavery
http://school.discoveryeducation.com/schooladventures/slavery/
Visitors to this site can learn about the history of slavery throughout the world and experience a slave auction.

A History of Slavery for Kids
http://people.historyforkids.org/slaves.htm
This site presents an account of the history behind slavery in ancient times as well as slavery in the United States.

History of Slavery in America Timeline
http://www.factmonster.com/timelines/slavery.html
This timeline lists key dates in the history of slavery in the United States.

PLACES TO VISIT

African Burying Ground Memorial Park
http://www.africanburyinggroundnh.org
1 Junkins Ave., Portsmouth, New Hampshire
Although the memorial is not yet built, posted signs make note of the burial ground located here.

African Burial Ground National Monument
http://www.nps.gov/afbg/index.htm
Ted Weiss Federal Building, 290 Broadway, New York, New York
The museum located at the site of the African American Burial Ground is a must-see. The memorial to these people is located behind the building and is an oasis of quiet in the midst of New York City's busy streets.

New York State Museum
http://www.nysm.nysed.gov
222 Madison Ave., Albany, New York
The New York State Museum has a display about the burial ground found at Schuyler farm. The reconstructed faces will be on exhibit in the future.

Onandaga Historical Association
http://www.cnyhistory.org/
321 Montgomery St., Syracuse, New York
An exhibit on the role Syracuse played in the Underground Railroad includes clay replicas of the faces of three escaped slaves.

Whitney Plantation
http://www.whitneyplantation.com
5099 Highway 18, Wallace, Louisiana
While other plantations in the southern US offer tours as well, the Whitney Plantation grounds and museum have a unique focus on the lives of the slaves that worked and lived here from the mid-1700s to the Civil War era.

INDEX

ABOUT THE AUTHOR

Lois Miner Huey is an archaeologist for the State of New York. She also writes nonfiction articles and books for kids, focusing on history and archaeology. Her most recent book was *Ick! Yuck! Eew! Our Gross American History*. Huey lives near Albany, New York, in a very old house with her archaeologist husband and three wonderful cats.